A NOTE TO PARENTS ABOUT GOSSIPING

Gossip is an age-old game played by a group of people sitting in a line or circle. One player whispers a message to his or her neighbor who whispers it to the next person. This continues until the last person repeats the message to the entire group. Without fail, the final message is vastly different from the original one. And so it is with real-life gossip. A verbal message passed from one person to another is, more often than not, distorted by the process. In the end, a message conveyed via gossip is not usually an accurate representation of the facts.

Facts distorted by gossip can be destructive. Therefore, gossiping is dangerous social behavior that needs to be avoided. The purpose of this book is to teach children how gossiping can be harmful and how it can and should be avoided.Reading and discussing this book with your child can prevent him or her from gossiping and becoming entangled in the uncomfortable situations that gossiping can create.

Your child will most likely follow your lead. If you do not want your child to gossip, you must not gossip. In addition, you need to redirect your child's conversation whenever he or she engages in gossip. Encourage your child to follow the old adage, "If you can't say something nice about someone, don't say anything at all."

This book belongs to:

_____

Published by Scholastic Inc.
90 Old Sherman Turnpike, Danbury, CT 06816.

SCHOLASTIC and associated logos are trademarks and/or
registered trademarks of Scholastic Inc.

ISBN 0-7172-8590-1

First Scholastic Printing, October 2005

A Book About
Gossiping

by **Joy Berry**

SCHOLASTIC INC.

New York   Toronto   London   Auckland   Sydney
Mexico City   New Delhi   Hong Kong   Buenos Aires

This book is about Katie and her friends Laura and Tommy.

Reading about Katie and her friends can help you understand and deal with **gossiping.**

You are gossiping when you tell others
unkind things about someone.

You are gossiping when you tell others untrue things about someone.

Gossiping can hurt the people you gossip about.

The things you say may cause them to feel bad about themselves.

The people you gossip about can be hurt in another way.

The things you say may cause others to treat them unkindly.

Gossiping can hurt you. If you say unkind things, people might think you are unkind. They might not like you. They might not want to be with you.

Gossiping can hurt you in another way. Others might think you are dishonest if what you say is not true. They might not trust you. They might not believe anything you say.

Gossiping can hurt others and it can hurt you. Do not gossip. Here is a good rule for you to follow:

If you cannot say something nice, do not say anything at all.

Some people may ask you questions about other people so that you will gossip. Do not gossip when this happens. Do these things instead:

- Explain kindly that you would rather not answer questions about others.
- Then suggest that you talk about something else.

Do not try to get other people to say things that are unkind or untrue.

Do not ask questions that will cause them to gossip.

Do not listen to people who want to gossip.
Do these things instead:
- Tell them kindly that you do not want to hear gossip.
- Go away from them if they continue gossiping.

You might feel hurt or angry when people gossip about you. You might want to gossip about them.

When people gossip about you, don't gossip about them. Do these things instead:

- Talk to them kindly. Ask them to stop gossiping about you.
- Try to work out your problems together. You may need to ask someone to help you.

You might feel like gossiping about people you do not know very well. Do not gossip about them. Do these things instead:

- Introduce yourself to the people.
- Get to know them and be kind to them.

It is important that you treat other people the way you want to be treated.

If you do not want people to gossip about you, you should not gossip about them.